ANIMAL FAMILIES

Kangaroos

NOEL SIMON

illustrated by Terry Riley

J. M. Dent & Sons Limited

London   Melbourne   Toronto

Commended by IUCN (International Union for Conservation of Nature and Natural Resources)

First published 1979
Text © Noel Simon 1979
Illustrations © J. M. Dent & Sons Ltd 1979
Reproduced and printed in Denmark by Grafodan Offset
for J. M. Dent & Sons Limited
Aldine House, Welbeck Street, London
This book is set in 14 on 16 pt Imprint 101
ISBN 0 460 06840 7

British Library Cataloguing in Publication Data
Simon, Noel
    Kangaroos.—(Animal families).
    1. Kangaroos—Juvenile literature
    I. Title   II. Riley, Terry   III. Series
    599'.2   QL737.M35

ISBN 0-460-06840-7

Contents

An adult red male is among the largest and most splendid of all the kangaroos

Introducing the Kangaroo

You may think that there is only one type of kangaroo. In fact there are many different kinds—about forty-five species altogether. Some of them have strange names—quokka, wallaroo, potoroo. Like the word kangaroo itself, these are names used by the Aborigines, Australia's original native people. Others have been given English names—rat-kangaroo, hare-wallaby, and the like—because they reminded the early settlers of familiar animals they had known in Europe. But they are not related, even remotely, to any European animal.

There is no difference between kangaroos and wallabies. The largest are the male grey and red kangaroos. When standing fully erect they are as tall as a man. The smallest are the rat-kangaroos, which are no larger than a small cat.

Males and females of the larger kangaroos are easily distinguished from one another. Not only is the female much smaller —less than half the size of the male—but some species also differ in coloration: the coat of the male red kangaroo, for example, is rusty brown, while the female's is blue-grey.

The kangaroo has very powerful hindlegs. They are much more highly developed than the forelimbs, or arms. The kangaroo's hindfoot is very long. It has only four toes. Of these, the middle toe is extremely large; it is tipped with a heavy claw and thickly padded underneath. The outer toe is small. The two inner toes are also small, and are joined together by a fold of skin so that they look like a single toe with twin nails.

Apart from its massive hindlegs, the kangaroo's most conspicuous feature is its huge tail, which helps to balance the animal as it travels at speed. When standing still or moving slowly the tail is used for a different purpose: it then becomes another limb, serving as a prop—rather like the third leg of a three-legged stool. This enables the kangaroo to squat firmly on its tail while leaving its arms free.

Kangaroos and other marsupials are distinguished from all other animals by a pouch—the *marsupium*, which gives the marsupials their name. This is a fold of skin on the lower part of the female's stomach, covering her nipples, which serves as a pocket in which the newborn young can develop in safety.

The adult male is called a buck; or, if he is an old man of the larger species, a 'boomer'. The adult female is called a doe, or a 'flyer'. The young is called a 'joey'. The herd is known as a 'mob'.

Where the Kangaroo Lives

Kangaroos are found all over Australia and Tasmania. Some also live in New Guinea and on a few other smaller islands.

As a group, the kangaroos are mainly grass-eating animals which are specially adapted for living in a hot climate. They have to survive not only high summer temperatures—often more than 40°C.—but also a long dry season. To do this they have to be capable of going for long periods with little or no water, at a time when pastures—never lush at the best of times—are at their least productive.

Kangaroos of one kind or another live in almost all the different types of habitat that Australia has to offer. Of the large species, the grey kangaroos inhabit forests and fairly dense bushland—not closed forests with dense stands of trees, but the open forests, grass-floored and with trees relatively widely scattered, which are so characteristic of much of the Australian bushlands. The antelope kangaroo is found in the more open country of northern Australia; the red kangaroo—one of the most widely distributed of all the kangaroos—on the open grass-lands; and the wallaroo, or euro, among the drier, rocky parts of the interior, where few other animals could exist.

One of the kangaroos' methods of coping with the problem of living in a very hot climate is to be active mainly by night. During the day they rest. The hotter the day the less active they will be. The tiny musky rat-kangaroo is the only kangaroo that is not nocturnal. Another of the rat-kangaroos escapes the heat by digging underground burrows.

But most kangaroos avoid the sun simply by sheltering in the shade of trees or clumps of bushes. Shelter is an important factor: in summer kangaroos need to shelter from the sun; in winter from the wind.

The Variety of Kangaroos

The smallest of the kangaroos are the rat-kangaroos. Apart from the little musky rat-kangaroo, which differs in many ways from all the others, they are divided into two groups: the bettongs and the potoroos.

The bettongs are generally associated with the drier areas. They are strictly nocturnal, taking care not to emerge from hiding until after dark, and to return long before the sun rises. Bettongs build nests on the ground. They make their nests of grass which they carry in little bundles in their tails. After biting off the individual blades of grass, they pick them up in their mouths, lay them on the ground, and with their hind feet push them backwards towards the tip of their tail, which is curled around to receive it.

The potoroos, on the other hand, have chosen to live in the higher rainfall areas where the vegetation is much denser. Adequate cover is very important to potoroos. They take care never to leave it, not even to feed. They need the cover as protection from their enemies. Being small animals, they are much more vulnerable to predation than the larger kangaroos, particularly to birds of prey, snakes, and some of the introduced predators—foxes, cats, and the like.

The hare-wallabies, which live on the grassy plains of inland

Rock wallabies can make spectacular leaps

Australia, are only a little bigger than the rat-kangaroos. They are called hare-wallabies because of their habit of making nests on the ground beneath tufts of grass or under bushes. When alarmed they burst out at tremendous speed, reminding the early settlers of the European hare. They also perform astonishing leaps.

Among the most interesting are the rock-wallabies, some of which have very distinctive coloration. On open ground the rock-wallaby resembles any other wallaby, though a closer look will show that its tail is tipped with long tufted hair. This helps provide a more delicate balance than other wallabies would find necessary. And their feet have extra thick pads with specially roughened surfaces to give a sure grip.

On the ground, the rock-wallaby's movements are awkward, almost clumsy. But among the rocks, boulders and cliffs which are its home it becomes completely transformed. It performs leaps which would do credit to a mountain goat, jumping from boulder to boulder with effortless ease and soaring across gullies and canyons with incredible grace. In climbing the sheer face of a cliff it leaps from one ledge to another as nimbly as any chamois or klipspringer, where the slightest error of judgement could cause it to be dashed on to the rocks or raging surf hundreds of feet below.

Tree kangaroos—living only in the forests of northern Queensland and New Guinea—are kangaroos which, in the course of evolution, have moved from the ground up into the trees. In the process they have developed special characteristics to fit them for life in the trees. Their feet are shorter than those of other kangaroos, their forelimbs relatively larger, and they have sharp claws, all of which help in moving along branches.

How Kangaroos avoid Competition

Where several different kinds of kangaroos live in the same general area they do not compete with one another; for, although living close together, each species is separated from the others by different habitat requirements and food preferences.

The red kangaroo, for example, closely resembles the antelope kangaroo—so closely that it is difficult to tell them apart. Yet the two species eat different types of vegetation. The red kangaroo likes short, green grasses and herbs. The antelope kangaroo, on the other hand, prefers the tall, coarser grasses. So the two species can live close together without competing.

Similarly, the red kangaroo is generally confined to the plains, whereas the euro, or wallaroo, prefers the uplands. While the red kangaroo limits itself to grazing, the euro mainly browses—that is feeds on the leaves and shoots of bushes, including the prickly leaves of spinifex. So these two species can live together without their interests clashing.

Some kangaroos live in the trees

Even when two grazing species live side by side, the same principle applies. The red kangaroo and the eastern grey kangaroo, for instance, are both grass-eaters. But they eat different types of grasses.

How the Kangaroo Moves

The kangaroo is the native grassland animal of Australia. It occupies the place that in other continents is filled by quite different types of grass-eating animals, such as the antelopes and gazelles of Africa, the deer of Eurasia, and the bison of North America.

Like all grass-eating animals, the kangaroos have evolved the means of moving rapidly over the ground. But they have done so in an altogether unusual manner. When feeding or moving slowly they crawl on all-fours with the full length of their feet on the ground. Both arms move forward together. While the feet are moving forward—also together—the animal supports its weight on its tail and on its forepaws. The exception is the tree kangaroo. In the trees each foot moves independently of the other—though on the ground it moves like any other kangaroo.

As the kangaroo gathers speed its method of movement

15

changes. Instead of running on all-fours, it hops. Leaning its body slightly forward, the kangaroo rises off its feet on to the tips of its toes. Both feet move forward together. It no longer uses its arms, but holds them close to its chest. The heavy tail extended behind serves to balance the upper parts of the body. The faster the animal moves the more its tail is extended.

Hopping may seem a curious way of moving, but it is highly effective: an adult male red kangaroo can cover the ground as fast as a racehorse. Females with pouch young naturally have difficulty in reaching the same high speeds as the males. At top speed the male covers about three metres at a bound; but much greater distances have been recorded. The record is held by a kangaroo chased by dogs which cleared 8.25 metres in a single hop, in the process leaping over a pile of timber 3 metres high. But kangaroos do not move fast unless forced to do so. They tire quickly, and much prefer to save their energies.

While one kangaroo crawls slowly on all-fours, another hops along

Birth

The main difference that distinguishes the marsupials from the more advanced—or placental—mammals is in their method of reproduction. In the placental mammals development of the foetus, the unborn young, inside the mother continues to an advanced stage, whereas the marsupial foetus is only partly developed inside its mother: it completes its development in the pouch.

The main advantage of the pouch is that it enables the new-born young—which is even more helpless than the newborn placental young—to develop in safety. It remains in the closest possible contact with its mother while leaving her free to concentrate entirely on feeding herself. Under the harsh conditions of Australia where food is seldom plentiful, this is naturally a very important consideration, not only for the mother but for her offspring as well.

The young is born after a very short gestation—the period of development inside its mother. Even the largest kangaroo has a gestation period of only thirty-three days. The newborn red kangaroo, for example—one of the largest of the kangaroos—is so tiny that it weighs less than 1 gm and is only 2 cm long. At birth its head and forearms are comparatively well developed. Its mouth, tongue and nose are large; though its eyes and ears are covered with a thin skin. Its hindlegs, on the other hand, have not begun to develop.

Yet this tiny, helpless, under-developed embryo manages without any help from its mother to find its way into her pouch. Its only guide is a trail of saliva which the mother lays across

her own stomach—though there is some doubt whether this is of any help to the embryo. It seems more likely that the mother's licking is simply part of the process of cleaning the pouch—which she does shortly before the birth—and has no other significance. When the young is in the pouch the female also frequently licks both pouch and young.

The only certain help the female gives is to adopt a special 'birth position'. Supporting her back against a tree, she takes the weight of her body on her tail, stretching out her legs in front of her, and leaning the upper part of her body forward.

The embryo wriggles towards the pouch as though swimming. It pulls itself forward by its arms and fingers. It gets no help from its hindlegs, for they are almost non-existent. Despite its evident helplessness, the embryo reaches the pouch in a surprisingly short time—usually within about three minutes from the moment of birth.

As soon as the embryo enters the pouch it clamps its mouth to a nipple—of which there are four. The nipple then swells in its mouth to the extent that it is very difficult to remove. And it remains firmly attached to the nipple until it is well developed.

With her back against a tree trunk, a female red kangaroo prepares to give birth

The Pattern of Reproduction

The red kangaroo's system of reproduction is so arranged that within two days of giving birth the female mates again. But the fertilized egg, or blastocyst as it is called, remains dormant— that is, does not start to develop—until about a month before the joey, already in the pouch, is ready to leave. As the joey remains in the pouch until it is 235 days old, this means that the blastocyst lies dormant for more than six and a half months.

As soon as the pouch is left empty by the previous occupant, a new birth takes place. Within a day or so of birth the female mates again and the cycle is repeated.

So it is perfectly normal for an adult female red kangaroo to have dependent young at three different stages of development at the same time: an unweaned juvenile which has recently left her pouch but is still suckling, a developing young in her pouch, and a fertilized egg—the blastocyst—lying dormant inside the mother awaiting the signal to start developing.

If the pouch young is accidentally lost the cycle is advanced and the blastocyst immediately starts to develop to take its place and make good the loss.

A joey being turned out of the pouch by its mother

Leaving the Pouch

The first time the joey leaves the pouch is normally the result of being deliberately turned out by his mother. His immediate reaction is to try to climb back in again; but this is prevented by his mother standing erect. It is then impossible for him to get in. At first he does not know what to do with his feet, for he has never used them before. He keeps falling over them. However, as he gains experience he learns to use them properly.

From the security of his mother's pouch the joey shows no sign of fear. But once he has left it he becomes rather nervous. A burst of birdsong or the crash of wings, the rustle of wind in the trees or a breaking twig will cause him to rush to his mother and frantically try to climb back into the only refuge he knows. But without his mother's cooperation he cannot do so. If she

*A timid joey hides
its head in its
mother's pouch*

declines to lower her body to allow him to enter, he may simply thrust his head into the pouch while his feet remain on the ground. This is enough to reassure him, and his confidence is soon restored. Even then he does not go far from his mother. He takes care to keep close to her, following her whenever she moves.

But if the danger is real, the mother reacts quite differently. She summons the youngster with a series of warning noises— made by drawing in her breath—at the same time leaning her body forward to bring the entrance of the pouch closer to the ground. The joey wastes no time in tumbling in head first. Once inside, a quick somersault aided by a few kicks and squirms turns him around until his head appears uppermost.

If caught unawares with no time for the joey to get back into her pouch, the female may have to abandon him. If at all possible she will return to collect him when the danger has past. But if she has been chased a long way, she may be unable to do so.

Growing Up

At first the doe shows little interest in her offspring. Not until the joey is able to move in and out of her pouch—which happens when it is about six months of age—do her maternal instincts assert themselves. She then becomes very devoted.

From the age of about five months the joey starts to poke his head out of the pouch and take a mild interest in his surroundings. Then, during his final month of pouch life, he begins to leave the pouch and experiment with eating grass. To start with he leaves the pouch only briefly: but each time he remains outside a little longer until, when nearly eight months old—235 days to be precise, if a red kangaroo—he leaves the pouch altogether.

The days of the joey's carefree existence are now over. When the doe realizes that she is ready once again to give birth she deliberately prevents him from entering her pouch, for she knows that he would accidentally kill the new young. But although denying him the use of her pouch, she nevertheless continues to allow him to suckle from outside. This goes on until the joey is finally weaned about four months later.

These first few months out of the pouch are a critical time in the young kangaroo's life. Though still reliant on his mother as his main source of food and protection, she can no longer give him her undivided attention. And as she now has two young to feed instead of only one, she has to work even harder at grazing in order to produce sufficient milk for them both. The joey remains so dependent on his mother for food that if he should become accidentally separated from her he could not survive on his own.

Instead of his nights being spent in the warmth and safety of his mother's pouch, the joey now has to learn to fend for himself. Apart from the cold, it is easier to become separated from his mother in the dark. Should he do so, there are often foxes and other predators lurking in the offing ready to pounce on any defenceless young animal.

Even when weaned, the joey continues to remain fairly close to his mother until he becomes mature. When that stage is reached—usually between about eighteen months and two years

A large joey continues to suckle from outside the pouch

of age—the young females are gradually absorbed into the mob, ready to start their own families, while the young males gather together in small bachelor groups, biding their time to mate

Until independence the young females have been the same size as males of their own age. But the young bucks now begin to outgrow them. They become taller, heavier, and much more muscular. Their arms become relatively longer and their chests broader. Their temperament changes at the same time: they become haughty and stand-offish.

Red kangaroo females are fully grown by the age of about five years. But the males continue to grow until they are about eight years old. Even after that the bucks continue to put on weight.

Social Life

Most grazing animals which gather together in numbers for mutual protection have a well developed social order. By acting as a group each individual animal benefits. But this does not apply to the kangaroos. Their social order is of a very primitive kind.

Though large numbers may sometimes gather loosely together, and remain together all day, they do so more by chance than deliberate choice. When several groups intermingle, giving the impression of being one large mob, they continue to act as individuals, never as a herd. Whatever happens, each animal thinks only of itself, and acts accordingly. This is especially noticeable when danger threatens: the mob then breaks up into a mass of individuals tearing away in every imaginable direction.

Except for the bond between the mother and her young, all kangaroo relationships are casual in the extreme. One or more males form a temporary association with any female that is ready to mate. But these associations are very brief—seldom more than a day at most. During that time the male is very attentive to the female; but for the greater part of the time he ignores her. Once he has mated, the male loses all interest in the female.

Mating generally takes place at night. The buck may remain close to the doe for a while after sun-up, occasionally uttering soft clucking sounds of endearment and at intervals sniffing her. But as the day becomes warmer he moves away to rest in the shade.

A cockatoo alerts a mob of red kangaroos to danger

The Day's Routine

As the first glow of dawn proclaims the start of a new day the kangaroos leave their main grazing zone, where they have spent the night, and return to their daytime resting area. They arrive singly or in twos and threes. Once the sun has risen above the horizon the mob gradually assembles. Mothers start the day by emptying the joeys from their pouches.

While some of the females graze intermittently—for with young to support they need to feed well—the males bask in the early morning sunshine. After the cold of the previous night they like to squat with half-closed eyes waiting for the warmth of the sun to dry their dew-soaked fur. The sun moves rapidly upwards, and by mid-morning—often earlier—the day is hot.

The day is a time for rest. During the dry season in particular kangaroos spend most of the day resting. Each animal chooses a patch of shade. Some species—the red kangaroo, for instance—like to dig hollows under trees or bushes for keeping cool and as dust baths. The bucks lie stretched out on the ground fully relaxed, sleeping in a series of short naps—sound sleep as we know it is rare in the animal world. They allow very little to disturb them. But if a buck should become alarmed he leaps into the air, thumping the ground with his hindfeet as he lands, at the same time uttering a loud warning cough.

The does are much more nervous than the bucks. Their ears constantly revolve like radar scanners to catch the slightest sound. They rely more on hearing than on eyesight. The least disturbance will bring them to their feet in a flurry of anxiety. The females' watchfulness ensures that the mob is always alert, ready to move off on the instant if disturbed or alarmed.

At intervals one or other of the mob will indulge in a scratching session, for the attentions of biting insects are a constant source of irritation. Leaning back on their tails, their eyes partly closed, the bucks methodically scratch themselves with their

Adult red kangaroos rest and doze during the heat of the day

Grey kangaroos watering at dusk

long foreclaws. It is obvious that scratching gives kangaroos enormous relief and great satisfaction.

The more delicate scratching calls for footwork. This is done not with the massive central toe, but with the pair of small inner toes which are ideal for grooming the fur and are used rather in the manner of a comb. Teeth and tongue are also brought into play for nibbling and licking.

As dusk approaches the mob becomes more active and starts to move into the open. Dusk is the main time for watering— though the mob may drink at other times if water is available. Kangaroos are always rather nervous when watering. They approach the waterhole cautiously, drink, and move off as quickly as they can. The night is spent feeding. At dawn they return again to their resting area. This routine changes with the weather. When the weather is cool they may feed throughout the day, pausing occasionally to rest.

As long as food and water are available, kangaroos are content to stay in one place, but when living conditions become difficult —as in times of drought—they move in search of food and water. Movement often follows rain, for rain brings a flush of new green growth which attracts kangaroos from a long way away.

30

Play

All young animals are naturally playful. The young kangaroo is no exception. The joey's first playmate is his mother.

The day starts with the joey installed in his mother's pouch. His mother keeps him there until the sun's rays have dispelled the cold night air and dried the dew from the grass. The joey's head protrudes from the pouch. He gazes about him rather unenthusiastically. As his mother leans forward to graze, he cranes his neck a little to reach the grass, nibbling at it in a rather half-hearted manner.

When the sun's warmth begins to be really felt, the doe pauses in her feeding long enough to give the joey his morning bath. She licks as much of him as she can while he is still in the pouch. Perhaps she finds it easier to control him that way. But there are parts of him she cannot reach, so she places her paws underneath the pouch and tips him bodily out. A few final licks and the morning's ablutions are complete. Then while the joey stands idly scratching himself, the doe quickly cleans out her pouch, which she takes care always to keep spotlessly tidy.

The joey meanwhile is looking around for some way to amuse himself. He hurls himself at his mother and wrestles with her. His patient mother gently restrains him with her arms, or controls him by holding him against her legs with her muzzle. Only very rarely does she scold or slap him.

The joey wriggles free and rushes off to play with another youngster of his own age. But he soon tires of that—nothing holds his interest for long—and dashes back to his mother who has resumed her feeding. She nuzzles him briefly.

Most of his play revolves around his mother. He skips about, brushing against her chest or jumping up at her, biting her ears or any other part of her that he can reach. But play makes him thirsty: at intervals he pauses long enough to thrust his head into her pouch to drink.

When the doe wishes to move she summons the joey with indrawn breath. He follows at her heels, keeping as close to her as he can, bouncing up and down in a series of quick hops rather like a jack-in-the-box in the grass.

The does are very indulgent even of joeys that are not their own. At the most they will push a strange joey away. But the attitude of the adult males is very different. Any joey rash enough to try to be too familiar with a buck is liable to receive a cuff that will send him sprawling.

A joey grazing from its mother's pouch

Fighting

Kangaroos are peaceful animals. Even the adult males are not aggressive unless seriously provoked. Normally the male kangaroo is completely indifferent to other animals. His movements are deliberate and dignified; and he treats other members of the mob with disdain. Rather like the African lion, he gives the impression of boredom and idleness.

Males meeting one another may rise up on their toes, like ballet dancers on their points, and indulge in a little mild sparring; yet despite exchanges of coughs and grunts, fighting is generally avoided. Serious fighting does not occur except when the male feels himself to be threatened. This is most likely to happen when a female is ready to be mated or when a strange male appears. Tempers then tend to become strained, and the normally placid male becomes transformed.

Among red kangaroos, a fight begins when one male challenges another by moving towards him in a series of short hops, holding his body upright. The two rivals crane their heads cautiously forward until their noses almost touch. One suddenly rises erect, reaching to his full height by standing on the tips of his toes and tail. Folding his arms in front of his chest, he swings his head from side to side, at the same time licking and biting the hair on his own chest. All the time he utters a series of clucks and warning coughs.

When males fight they rise on their toes and use their arms like flails

A red kangaroo male kicks out at his opponent

If this display fails to deter his opponent, the challenger may drop on to all-fours, spreading his limbs as wide as possible, and carrying the weight of his body on the tips of his arms, legs and tail. His body quivers with indignation. Should the other accept the challenge, he rears up in his turn. The two animals circle about like boxers searching for an opening in their opponents' defences. They sway backwards and forwards, grappling with their arms, each striving to lift the other off the ground. When that fails, they use their claw-tipped arms like flails, aiming at each other's faces, in particular at the eyes and ears. Keeping their heads well back out of reach, they fend off blows with their arms, at the same time prancing about searching for an opportunity to deal a powerful swipe.

36

Suddenly one leans back on his tail and, raising both feet together, aims a vicious kick at his rival's stomach. The other tries to turn this to his own advantage by catching his opponent off balance and hurling him to the ground. The fight then degenerates into a kicking match, each attempting to rip the other with his feet.

Before long both have had enough. They either give up and turn away or drop on to all-fours and without further ado start grazing together as though on perfectly friendly terms.

Enemies

Until about two centuries ago the kangaroos and other marsupials had the Australian continent more or less to themselves. For millions of years they had lived and evolved in isolation without competition from more advanced animals.

The arrival of the first people—the Aborigines—altered this situation. Apart from themselves hunting the kangaroos, the Aborigines brought with them the dingo—a tawny-yellow dog, which started as a domestic animal, but later went wild. But, although the Aborigines lived by hunting, there were not many of them, their weapons were simple, and they hunted only for food. So their impact on the native animals was not very serious.

Dingos hunting either singly or in packs are perfectly capable of killing kangaroos. But although they kill young kangaroos, they are likely to be wary of attacking the adult males. A big boomer can be a formidable opponent. His arms though less powerful than his legs are nonetheless very strong as well as being tipped with knife-sharp claws.

If attacked by a pack of dingos the female kangaroo's best means of defence lies in flight; but the male prefers to stand and fight. A buck kangaroo with his back to a tree or large boulder can give a very good account of himself. A dingo coming within range of his hindlegs is liable to be raked by sharp claws. Should the dingo be so unwise as to leap at the buck's throat, the kangaroo will respond by clasping his attacker in his arms and tearing at him with clawed feet. If a waterhole or stream is close at hand, a boomer attacked by a pack may take refuge in it. Any dingo entering the water is seized by the kangaroo and either held beneath the surface or trampled underfoot until it drowns.

But dingos do not often attack boomers: they find it easier to scavenge. And in a continent where native scavengers are scarce, they have little difficulty in obtaining all the food they want. There are in any event many other kinds of smaller marsupials which are easier for them to hunt. So there is no reason why they should bother to attack the boomers.

Among the larger kangaroos the danger from disturbance is probably greater than from predation. If the females are disturbed and forced to flee it is very easy for the joeys to be thrown from the pouch and lost.

A pack of dingos on the look out for prey

How Numbers are Controlled

Nature's way of controlling the numbers of kangaroos is through the pouch young. Although under normal conditions breeding among kangaroos is a more or less continuous process, reproduction is governed by the availability of suitable food. This, in turn, is controlled by the rainfall.

In times of plenty breeding progresses satisfactorily. Each adult female—as we have seen—can have one young in the pouch and another at foot. As long as food is abundant the females can provide adequate milk, the joeys will flourish, and most will grow into adults. And if a joey should die there is always another ready to come forward to take its place.

But in a poor year when drought brings starvation, losses will be heavy. The mother's milk is reduced, and the joey dies. Although its place is taken by another, it will survive only if conditions improve. The worse the climatic conditions the more joeys will die. In times of severe drought the mother's milk dries up completely, all joeys die and breeding ceases altogether. This leaves the female free to concentrate exclusively on her own survival, to be ready to breed again as soon as suitable conditions return.

This may seem a rough and ready way of controlling the kangaroo population. But in the absence of predators it is highly effective, in that it achieves the essential purpose of keeping the numbers of kangaroos in balance with their environment.

And as the condition of the environment changes according to the climate, nature's system of control causes the numbers of kangaroos to vary quite rapidly to meet changing conditions.

Because breeding under good conditions continues almost without pause, a fresh new crop of young can quickly appear to make up previous losses. Even when severe drought has halted all breeding, the change can occur surprisingly rapidly. Within a month of the drought being broken by rain and a flush of green vegetation appearing, reproduction is once again in full swing.

Nature also exercises control over numbers by regulating the age at which young kangaroos can start to breed. If weather conditions are right and food freely available, the female red kangaroos mature relatively early and are able to breed from the age of about eighteen months (males from the age of about twenty-eight months). If, on the other hand, conditions are poor, maturity will be delayed, possibly until the females are four, or even five, years of age.

Drought kills off large numbers of kangaroos

Conserving the Kangaroo

For millions of years the kangaroo and other marsupials had had Australia almost to themselves. But during the nineteenth century the continent became dominated by man and his domestic livestock.

In addition to cattle and sheep, other kinds of animals, which had not previously existed in Australia, were brought in to the country. Among them were cats, dogs, pigs, goats, horses, and even camels. Many of these domestic animals escaped from farms and houses into the bush and took to living wild.

The arrival of the rabbit was particularly disastrous. Numbers increased so rapidly that within a few years the rabbit had over-run the greater part of the continent. Millions of them swarmed over the land like locusts, eating every blade of grass, even destroying trees and bushes.

The rabbit has caused a great deal of damage to Australian vegetation

When the rabbit was seen to be getting out of hand, several of its natural enemies—foxes, ferrets, stoats and weasels—were turned loose in an attempt to control the horde. But they preyed instead upon the native marsupials and birds.

Meanwhile, much of the land was being developed for farming. All this greatly altered the character of the land and made a tremendous impact on the native animals. As if this were not enough, large numbers of kangaroos have in recent years been slaughtered for meat, much of it destined for pet food. Decline in the quality of the habitat and excessive shooting are the greatest threats to the various species of kangaroos.

Kangaroos of the arid country, such as the euro, are in little danger as they occupy land which is so poor that it is unlikely to be required for domestic livestock—though even there they may still need protection from over-hunting.

But as the country becomes more intensively developed for human use there can be no doubt that those species such as the red kangaroo which require richer pasturage are going to come under increasing pressures.

For some of the rarer species of kangaroos the best long term hope lies in special areas being set aside as reserves—in places where their presence will not conflict with man's interests. Such reserves would benefit not only the kangaroos but many of the smaller marsupials as well.

For the more common species, however, there is no reason why reasonable numbers of kangaroos should not be permitted to continue to live side by side with domestic livestock. It would be quite wrong to assume that destruction of the kangaroos will leave more pasturage for sheep. This is wrong because kangaroos and sheep each make different demands on the environ-

Kangaroos and sheep can live together without competing for grazing

ment so do not compete with each other to any great extent. They eat different types of grasses. They can therefore live together without the kangaroos depriving the sheep of grazing. Even if all the kangaroos were destroyed the sheep would not necessarily benefit. There is, in any event, room enough for both: and it is difficult to believe that Australians will not insist on adequate measures being taken to safeguard animals as uniquely Australian as the kangaroos.